C000102216

Master Dressage
The Basics

DEDICATION

We dedicate this volume of instruction to all the hardworking riders, coaches and owners of horses. Riding is a wonderful sport but it can also be frustrating and extremely hard work. We hope our words make your relationship with your horse more fulfilling than before.

THANK YOU

A big thank you goes to all Facebook fans of Master Dressage and Ride With Your Mind for all your support. We would also like to thank the following people for their help with editing, ideas, photos and feedback:

Emma Dove, Milly Dove, Linda Yeardley(editing), Mike Clark(editing), Karin Major, Pam Barker(editing) and Karen Nunwick(editing).

Thank you to all who have been involved in this book.

Printed by Evergood Ltd

CONTENTS

1 GROUND WORK

Introduction

Having a cohesive ground work strategy makes training your horse more efficient and straight forward. It provides a number of fall back points for difficult or tricky horses. Many ground work systems are either too basic or do not translate well to riding the horse. Systems which teach the horse to follow the handler's feet can often fail when the rider gets back on, since there are then no feet to follow!

My first introduction to the ground work system I (Peter) am about to describe was on a course at Overdale Equestrian Centre. As soon as I started working with the system and observing its effect on my own horse, I realised that this system was the tool I had been missing all this time. I was then lucky enough to begin filming the system for a DVD with Ali Wakelin (www.aliwakelin.co.uk) and Mary Wanless. This will be released soon.

The system was created by Dr. Andrew McLean who runs the Australian Equine Behaviour Centre and is the author of 5 books and 35 peer-review journal articles. The system has been further developed by Mary and Ali.

His website http://www.aebc.com.au contains a wealth of information and is well worth visiting.

The Basics

This system of ground work is designed to teach the horse to respond to clear signals which are then easily transferable to ridden work. The horse is taught to respond to these signals and not to follow the handler's feet. To this end, the horse must always move before you move and must always stop before you stop. This is one of the most important ideas in this system.

The Training Position

In the training position the handler should be facing the horse, so that she can watch his responses. Any forward movement of the horse will require the handler to step backwards. If the horse is slightly to your left as you face him, you hold the reins in your left hand, and the schooling whip in your right. You will need to work from both sides in your training.

The way you hold the reins is also very important, as you need to be able to apply pressure and release it easily. You also need to be able to move out to the end of the rein without losing control.

The buckle of the rein rests in the groove between your thumb and first finger. The bulk of the reins fall into a loop as you also hold the reins under the horse's chin, passing one between the thumb and first finger, and the other between the first and index finger. See photo 1. This allows us to apply pressure in a very controlled manner, then to easily release it as we back away from the horse and switch to just holding the buckle.

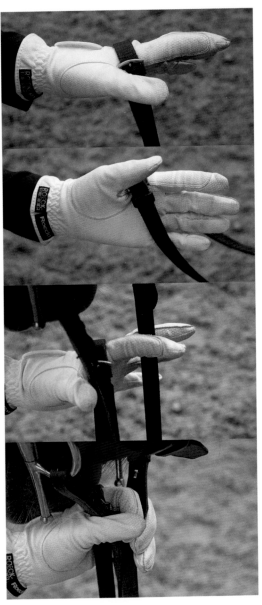

Photo 1 - How to hold the rein

Desensitisation

Before any further training work can begin the horse must be desensitised to the schooling whip. The horse must lose its fear of the whip and learn that it is an aid like any other. My daughter's horse Tinker used to react too much to the use of the schooling whip but now has a much more normal response after desensitisation work.

Photo 2 - Tinker is being desensitised to the schooling whip

First make sure you are in the training position. Then, starting at the neck and shoulders, stroke the length of the whip against your horse. See Photo 2 for an example. The whip should only be removed from the horse's body when he stops moving, otherwise you are rewarding the act of moving. You can eventually progress to stroking the flanks and rump. Be careful not to 'poke' or tickle the horse with the end of the whip. The aim is to have the horse relaxed and standing still as you stroke with the whip. This may take some time and effort depending on the sensitivity of your horse. Do not rush to get past this stage.

Head Lowering

The horse who has his head raised is in flight mode and lowering his head lowers his adrenaline levels, making him calmer and more receptive. To lower your horse's head, hold the reins as described and stand close to him, making a consistent downward pressure. 'Snake' your hand a little to left and right if he braces himself against you, but try not to brace your arm against him. The moment he lowers his head a little, release the pressure and if he raises his head begin again. Most horses will soon begin to lower their head more easily.

Stepping Back

Since your primary aim is to reduce or eliminate the horse's flight reflex, you next want to teach him to step back. You have been holding the whip in a forehand grip; think now of this becoming a backhand grip as you place the whip between your body and the horse's front legs.

Use a little backward pressure from your hand on the reins and tap lightly and quickly on one leg just below the knee. If the horse is wearing boots tap above the boots. Start by asking for single steps and as soon as he steps that leg back, stop tapping. Then tap on the other leg. Each step must happen only when asked for, as we do not want the horse shooting backwards. After each good response, step back yourself to hold the reins just with the buckle, and let him digest the information you have given him. If he sighs, yawns, licks his lips, chews the bit, or blinks rapidly, he is making mental/emotional adjustments. You will soon be able to move your horse back several steps by tapping on each leg in turn, and over time he will begin to step back easily and fluidly.

Photo 3 – Stepping Back

About Pressure

Imagine a scale of 0 to 5, where 0 is no pressure and 5 would be the amount of pressure you would apply to stop the horse from dragging you over the edge of a cliff! Most people spend their life at a 3 - whether on the ground or riding. We tend to use the same amount of rein or leg pressure even to the point of nagging continuously.

In this form of training it is important to be able to start with the lightest pressure and then escalate evenly until you get the correct response. The system uses 'pressure and release', applying just enough pressure to generate a response, and then releasing when you get the beginnings of that response. From the horse's perspective, he is using trial and error learning to find the response that will make you release that pressure!

This is the baseline of 'operant conditioning', a term used in behavioural psychology. It describes the use of negative reinforcement applied until the desired response, then an immediate removal of pressure. Research has shown that using negative reinforcement, along with clicker training to reinforce the release trains horses in the most deep and efficient way. (Riders too learn best through trial and error as they home in on the most helpful co-ordinations – and pupils like positive reinforcement too!)

Over time, you can gradually raise your standards, so instead of releasing for a 'basic attempt' you require a bigger step or more promptness. If we wish to train the horse to go from the lightest aids, then we must always start from those light aids and then escalate them as needed, knowing that our aim is to be able to use light pressure whenever possible. But if our repertoire still ranges from 0 - 5 we will be much clearer and more effective in our training.

Go

From halt, stand in the training position, and ask the horse to move forwards with the rein by moving your hand towards you. Then touch the horse with the whip where you would normally apply your leg aid. See photo 4 for a visual explanation of where to use the whip. If the horse does not walk forward immediately, replace the touch with a series of taps, gradually increasing the strength and speed of the taps until your horse walks on. In this way we keep escalating the pressure until your horse walks, at which point we stop tapping. Only ask for a few steps to start with so that you keep control of each step. Tinker, in the photo, walks on from a single touch most of the time.

Photo 4 - Touching the horse with the whip to walk on.

It is very important not to start walking backwards yourself until the horse has begun to move. He must make the first step, so that he learns to respond to your hand and the touch of the whip, and not simply to follow the handler's footsteps.

Stop

Stop is achieved by making a backward pressure on the reins, moving your hand back under the horse's chin whilst still walking backwards. Remember to start with the lightest pressure, and to increase this until the horse stops. The tricky part is to coordinate moving your hand forward whilst walking backwards. When your horse stops completely, you continue moving backwards until you are just holding the end of the rein.

Deletion

If your horse steps towards you as you do this, move towards him and use the whip on his front legs to step him back. Ideally, ask for the same number of steps that he took by mistake. When he halts, step away from him again.

This is an example of deletion, with the handler 'deleting' the extra steps she did not want the horse to take. Very soon the horse learns that the human has personal space and that he must not move into it unless directed.

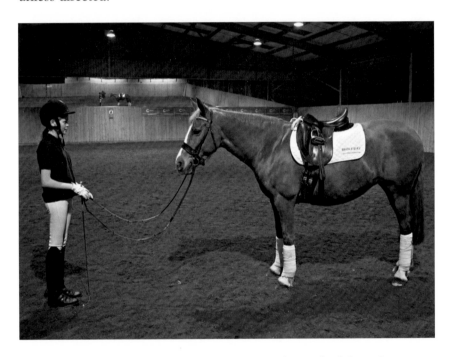

Photo 5 - The handler continues out on to the end of the rein.

Park

In Photo 5 you can see the horse is parked. The handler can test the security of the parking by moving left, right and even walking around each side to the horse's shoulder in an arc. A well trained horse should park, allowing the handler/rider to perform all manner of tasks. This kind of training helps enormously when at competitions in the lorry parking area and whilst mounting.

Summary

Improving your work on the ground will help to create a horse that is well mannered when handled and more sensitive to stop/go aids when mounted. This chapter is but the beginning of a much bigger project which aims to create a detailed DVD of this ground work system. There is more information about this on www.mary-wanless.com/ground-work.html - this will also address how to teach the horse to move his quarters over and step to the side with each front leg. For further information you can go to the http://www.aebc.com.au website

2 POSITION & ALIGNMENT

Shoulder, Hip, Heel

The word alignment covers a number of elements within skillful riding and for this short chapter we will cover the basics which need to be in place for a rider to have a chance of riding well.

The first question I (Mary) ask myself when I assess a rider is 'If I were to take the horse out from underneath the rider, as if by magic, how would she land on the arena?' Would she land on her feet, would she fall backwards, or would she fall forwards?

I also ask, 'Is her torso a vertical box, whose front has the same length as the back?' and 'Is the underneath of the box too short or too long, or does it take up the appropriate space between the front and back?' The former is one of the definitions of 'neutral spine', in which a person's spinal curves are in balance. In this position the spine is strongest and best placed to withstand the forces acting on it. In this alignment the rider's seat bones will point straight down.

If you sit on your hands using a firm chair placed sideways on to a large mirror, you can experiment to find 'neutral spine' whilst sitting. Experiment too with losing that box-shape by either hollowing your back (and pointing your seat bones back) and rounding your back (and pointing your seat bones forward). Move between these positions, gradually reducing their extremes, until you find the neutral place which makes your seat bones point straight down. Notice if you have a much bigger range of motion in one of those directions - this is likely to determine your 'default position' when you ride.

Photo 6 – Heather Blitz showing correct alignment

In the photo above, you can see Heather Blitz, a Grand Prix dressage rider and Pan American Gold Medalist, showing correct alignment. You can see that, if the horse were taken out from underneath her, she would land on her feet on the arena and then remain in that balance. It is her neutral spine and vertically aligned shoulder, hip, and heel that make this possible. Very few riders naturally sit like this. Their mid back (the lumbar spine between their ribs and their hips) acts as a hinge and becomes unstable, making their back round or hollow. Over time this can cause back pain, and many riders find that they become pain free once they adopt neutral spine.

As riders we want the hip joint and not the lumbar spine to act as the body's main hinge, and for the hip joint to keep making the small adjustments that keep the torso vertically aligned even when the horse accelerates or decelerates. Riders move the hip joint through its largest range of motion in rising trot and when they fold down over a jump. (Overall, though, we move it through a much smaller range of motion than most athletes and dancers, especially if we sit quietly and have good control of our seat bones move.) The lumbar spine is primarily involved in stabilising the torso so that the rider does not 'wiggle in the middle' whilst riding any of the gaits.

Leg position

Many riders who have been told to place their lower leg 'on the girth' are surprised when asked to bring it back underneath them, so that the knobble on the outside of their ankle is vertically under the boney knobble on their top outside. If you watch elite riders you will usually see this alignment, and indeed our traditional language of riding talks about the shoulder/hip/heel vertical line. Most riders, however, pay only lip service to the idea.

Riders are also often surprised when I adjust their stirrups so that their thigh bone lies at the 45 degree angle that is half way between horizontal and vertical. Many riders are riding with their stirrups too long, as they attempt to 'stretch their leg down'. Elite riders show the 45 degree thigh, or ride slightly longer than that, which I only recommend when your skills are well developed. At these angles the thigh can become part of your sitting surface, and when it is weight bearing, it spreads your weight forward over the horse's rib cage. This is much better for him than concentrating your weight in your seat, and thus on the small area of his back that he so easily hollows.

If your inner thigh is to be weight bearing, it has to be on the saddle. Again, if you look at photographs of elite riders riding towards the camera, you will always see their inside thigh on the saddle. Yet many riders are taught to 'relax the thigh and take it off the saddle'. Your sitting surface should extend down the whole of the suede surface on a pair of suede-seated breeches. Your thigh then acts as a lever, with the weight that acts at the knee end counterbalancing the weight of your torso that is stacked over the other end. Think of 80% of your weight in your thigh and 20% in your seat. Heather is demonstrating this in the photograph. She also has very little of her weight pushing into her stirrups. Her feet rest in them, rather than pressing into them, since this would create an equal and opposite upward force which could cause her joints to straighten, preventing them from acting as shock absorbers.

Supporting your body weight

The rider who sits 'like a sack of potatoes' does not use her thigh well, and also does not support her body weight. As she flops or presses down onto her horse he will almost certainly hollow his back underneath her. You probably know the difference between picking up a child who wants to be picked up and picking up one who makes herself into 'dead weight'. Skilled riders are like the child who wants to be picked up, and they sit as if they were suspended (in neutral spine) from a harness. Indeed, they master the art of picking the horse's back up under them, as if the horse were adhered to their breeches, so that lifting the harness picks him up too!

Your Mission

With the shoulder, hip, heel alignment and neutral spine set up, you might believe that the job is done. Nothing could be further from the truth! Once you add the horse jumping from one diagonal pair to the other in trot and bounding through each canter stride you will find yourself extremely occupied with the attempt to keep a strong and stable position! Position & alignment are a dynamic series of small adjustments which keep you in perfect balance with your horse. Many riders are anxious about not toppling forward and adding unnecessarily to the weight on the horse's forehand but most riders are behind the ideal balance point, not ahead of it.

Think of the horse like a space hopper (hippity-hop) balloon. As he 'hops' along under you, would you be pro-active enough to hop with him, or would you have to prevent yourself from falling off the back of him by pulling on the reins? Our primary aim as riders is to match the forces which the horse's movement exerts on our body, so that we are not 'left behind'. Only then can we push our hands forward instead of pulling back.

Your mission is to notice how the forces of the horse's movement could deform your body and to prevent that from happening, as Heather is doing in the photograph. So imagine, in contrast, a rider who is leaning back (from the hinge of the hip) whilst possibly also rounding or hollowing her back (from the hinge of the lumbar spine).

She already has her centre of gravity behind her horse's centre of gravity, forcing him to tow her along, and if he suddenly accelerated she would have to hang onto the reins even more to prevent herself from toppling backwards.

Whilst sitting in neutral spine get someone to put their thumb and first finger on each side of your sternum, just below your collar bone and between two of your upper ribs. Ask her to push you backwards and resist her push. Then ask her to put her hands in front of your hands, and give you a resistance to push your hands into. This will also help you to switch on the core strength of your bear down. Instead of being relaxed, you are ready to match the forces of the horse's movement and to prevent yourself from being deformed by those forces. The irony is that skilled riders who do this really well will probably tell you that they are 'doing nothing'!

Riders with back pain can become pain free once they discover how to ride in neutral spine. The next illustration shows some of the different ways in which a rider can lose neutral spine. We have kept the alignment of the lower leg virtually the same in all of them, but riders will exhibit larger variations than we have shown here.

1. Neutral spine and vertical.
2. Lean forward, still a box.
3. Lean back, still a box.
4. Hollow back, still vertical.
5. Round back, still vertical.
6. Hollow back and lean back (sophisticated hollow back*).
7. Round back and lean back.
8. Hollow back and lean forward.
9. Round back and lean forward.

* The sophisticated hollow back is often shown by experienced dressage riders, hence its name.

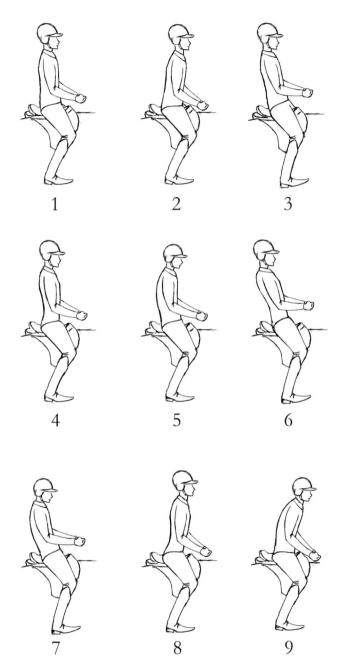

1

2

3

4

5

6

7

8

9

Figure 1

3 THE SEAT

Introduction

It is unfortunate that our traditional language of riding includes the terms 'drive your horse forward', 'use your seat', 'sit deep', 'push', and 'use your back'. These phrases are rarely explained and they can be interpreted in a multitude of ways, which usually involve the rider shoving with her seat and 'pushing' the saddle into the horse's back. However, the most skilled riders sit incredibly still; you do not see them shoving, pushing or grinding their seat into the horses back. They look like a carousel pole that is growing out of a carousel horse.

Basic Seat Bone Movement

When you are next riding your horse, notice what is happening to your seat bones: do they both move backwards and forwards at the same time, or do they move one at a time? If so, is this movement primarily a side to side movement, an up/down movement or a forward/backward movement? If you move both seat bones at the same time, you are almost certainly pushing with your seat, adding extra force that should not be there. Ideally, you want the movement of your seat bones to mould onto the movement of the horse's back and actually to influence that movement underneath you.

The muscles along the horse's back contract on one side and then the other. You can feel the equivalent of this in your own body if you place your fingers either side of your spine, and then start walking. You could feel this on your horse by placing your hands each side of his spine as someone else leads him in hand. The movement is much smaller than most people think it is. (Realise that you are not sitting on his shoulder blades!)

This one-side-at-a-time movement dictates that your seat bones should be moving separately. You want to feel them being carried forward one at a time, as if they were walking along, so the movement is primarily on the back/front plane. Each seat bone should make a small, repeatable movement that follows a track just inside the seam lines of the saddle, moving forward, up and in, almost like a horse with a bad front leg action that plaits (braids). Imagine a pencil point on each seat bone: what shape would these draw? Are they mirror images of each other? Is one a lighter line and one a deeper, darker line? Is each line repeatable or more random? Can you begin to change them? Most people have some weird quirks to the movement of at least one of their seat bones!

Controlling the Tempo in Walk

Make a 'guesstimate' of how much seat bone movement there actually is. Is it millimetres or centimetres; half an inch, or several inches? Large seat bone movements imply that you are either pushing them forcefully, or that you are being sloppy and that your muscles are too wobbly to control how your seat bones move. Thus both ends of that spectrum lead to seat bone movements that are too big. Realise that if you are a wobbly rider who is not controlling your seat bones then your horse is, and this gives him control of the speed of his legs. You may well be tempted to pull on the reins to slow him down but this does not work. Instead, you have to become the one who has control of the speed at which you move your seat bones, and thus the speed at which he moves his legs.

You have to restrict how much movement there is in each seat bone. The majority of riders have to halve the amount of movement they are making, and many have to halve it again. About one to two centimetres, or a half inch to an inch, is probably about right. Reducing it to this amount will require you to firm up around the thigh and pelvic muscles (if you are a wobbly rider) or reduce the force that you put into their movement (if you are a 'shovey' rider). If you have a horse who attempts to speed off in walk the movement may travel up your spine so that you move your waist and/or shoulders too. In that case you will have to work even harder at sitting still and reducing the wiggle.

Hind Leg Position

Having separated your seat bones, you are now in a position to know which hind leg is coming underneath you at any point. This takes a little bit of practice with someone on the ground, but you will soon increase your feel for it. Get someone on the ground to call 'now' as the hind leg starts to swing forward and see if you can match that up to where your seat bone is at the time.

As you make seat bone movement your focus, you will find that your horse will start to adjust its tempo and slow down, listening a lot more to your seat bones. Many riders are under the impression that they should allow their seat simply to 'go with' the horse. This notion, whilst poetic, will leave the rider no way to control the horse's tempo and no way to create impulsion or lengthen a horse's stride. To do either of the latter we have to ask for more energy whilst maintaining the same tempo, otherwise the horse would simply speed up his legs. This means that the rider must be able to move her leg from the knee down (i.e. to kick) with nothing changing from the knee up. (i.e. no wiggles, jiggles, shoves, or speeding, uncontrolled seat bones.) This is easier said than done!

Driving With the Seat

I (Peter) would like to attempt to provide an interpretation for this carelessly used phrase. Imagine that you are sitting in your car, driving down a nice, safe road. You decide to sit upright so that your back is no longer resting on the back of the seat. You are holding the steering wheel lightly and you feel stable - the name of the game here is to not let your back touch the seat. I would like you now to imagine what would happen to your body if you were to press hard on the accelerator.

For obvious safety reasons I do not recommend this experiment to anyone, but I have tried it myself. What I find is that if I do not 'do something' to prevent it, I will be left hanging onto the steering wheel attempting to keep my back from touching the seat. Similarly when an airplane accelerates down the runway, you would also have to work hard to prevent your body from being pushed back into the seat.

Now translate this to asking the horse to accelerate, perhaps by creating more impulsion, going from walk to canter or performing medium or extended paces. We are now in exactly the same situation and we must do something to prevent ourselves from hanging onto the 'steering wheel' and/or getting left behind. To keep up with the horse and remain independent of the reins I have to provide a force from the back of my body to the front of my body. This keeps me in charge of the position of my centre of gravity. I will have to feel as though I push the back of my body up towards the front of my body

18

and the front of my body forwards towards my hands. I will need to engage my core muscles to achieve this. To take the horse forwards like this is a wonderful feeling.

So let us reinterpret the idea of 'push' so that it does not suggest that you make pushing movements with your seat. Instead, it means that you activate your core as you would have to do to stop yourself from falling back against the car or airplane seat. Firstly, you pull your stomach in to make a wall (which Pilates teachers often call 'navel to spine') but then you also *push your guts against that wall* (realising that Pilates exercises are not done on a moving surface, hence this addition).

You naturally make a wall and push against it whenever you clear your throat, cough, or giggle. Try that now and add the sounds 'psshhht' and 'grrrrrr'. I (Mary) called this 'bearing down' when I first discovered it in the late 1970s. You may prefer the terms 'bear forward' or 'bear out'. None of them perfectly describe how you make a wall and push your guts against that wall - and there seems to be no really good term to describe this in any language! You would also bear down naturally if you put your knuckles against a wall whilst standing in a riding position and then pushed against that wall. Do that experiment now if you can (see photo 7).

Bearing down increases the pressure in your insides, and on a horse it stabilises your body so that you can match the forces of the horse's movement. Then, even during acceleration, you will not topple backwards and/or need to pull on the reins.

The push forward that you make with your bear down should always be stronger than the hold you have on the reins. This serves as a definition of 'riding the horse from back to front'. When your pull is stronger than your push you are 'riding him from front to back'. Charlotte Dujardin's riding is a masterclass in 'back to front' riding and pushing the hands forward, but realise that she can only do this because of the way in which she activates her core.

Photo 7 – Pushing against a wall

Weight Aids

I (Mary) do not talk about weight aids in discussions on turning or lateral work. I do not teach people to push down in one or both stirrups, or put weight on one seat bone. (Would this imply that the other one would lift and lighten?) Vague statements about the rider's weight leave too much room for misinterpretation.

The horse is undoubtedly affected by the position of the rider's centre of gravity, and as riders we are learning to control this. Weight aids do exist and effective ones happen naturally when you get your thighs, pelvis and torso stacked up correctly for the movement you are performing. In the section on turning you will hear more about how the positioning of your body can keep your centre of gravity in the appropriate place, giving you the influence you need.

4 STOP

When making a transition to halt from walk or trot, significant forces act on the rider, who could cause the rider to make a lot of mistakes. Since one of the aims of this book is to provide practical exercises you can try when riding, below is a list of questions you can ask yourself next time you make a downward transition from walk to halt. Think of this as training of the faculty of 'noticing'. Good riders notice their own body and that of the horse from moment to moment. They also question, and think about how cause and effect operates within the rider/horse interaction.

Ask yourself the following

1. What percentage of your tactics for halting has to do with your reins? Do the reins occupy all of your 'brain-space'?
2. As you come into the halt, does your upper body stay completely vertical, does it lean backwards or does it lean forwards? Do you hollow your back and grow taller, or do you round your back? Does your torso stay box-shaped? You may need a video to see this.
3. What happens to your seat bones when you halt? Do they become more or less clear? Do you push them down into the saddle? Do you push into your stirrups and make your seat bones lighten? Do your seat bones stop or keep moving?
4. Do your inside thighs become more snug against the saddle or do they come away from the saddle?
5. What happens to your stomach and core when you halt? Do you suck your stomach in? Do you let your guts hang out? Do you make a wall and push against that wall?

By asking these questions you will be able to uncover your current strategy for walk/halt transitions. This is probably your strategy for all downward transitions, with your mistakes being exaggerated - and having larger detrimental effects - as the downward transitions become more demanding. The information you glean will pinpoint your mistakes. This will bring to the surface of your mind what you need to pay attention to as you relearn how to ride transitions more effectively.

The basics of halting

After reading the chapter on the seat you hopefully have a good idea how of you can influence the tempo of the horse through control of the speed of your seat bones. You should also understand the importance of bearing down/forward/out, which helps to stabilise your torso as you match the forces generated by the horse.

To come into halt from walk, you will need to increase your bear down, bring your seat bones to a halt, hold your torso vertical, and make a passive resistance on the reins. The concept of passive resistance is explained in chapter 7 on Rein Aids. A good halt is like a knife going through butter; the horse does not dribble into halt, instead he takes three beats of his front legs to come to a deliberate stop. You are in effect stopping yourself, putting yourself into halt. Whilst you are stopping your seat bones and making a passive resistance through the reins you will need to work hard to keep your torso vertical and stable. As implied by the questions above, it could deform in a variety of ways.

How well your horse stops depends on a number of factors, one of them being the respect he has for the bit. You should use the ground work in Chapter 1 to get to a point where your horse will stop from the lightest contact on the rein. To transfer this to riding, you will need to have a good position, with good alignment that you maintain as you halt. You also need to have control of the speed of the horse's legs before you ask for the transition. Otherwise you and he will both pull on the reins as he fails to stop well.

The cost of leaning back in a walk-halt transition

One of the typical errors is leaning back, which is always associated with the rider pulling back on the reins rather than making a passive resistance. This puts her centre of gravity behind the horse's, which traps both of them in the waterski-motorboat dynamic. The horse will tow the rider along as both of them pull against each other. The same laws of physics make your skis speed out from under you if you lean back when skiing, but horses sometimes enact the principle in slow motion as they fail to halt.

The dynamics of leaning back mean you are more reliant on the reins than ever before - not only in the attempt to stop your horse, but also in preventing yourself from falling off backwards! Riders in this position often push their seat into the horse's back, which can cause it to hollow even more. So in response to a rider who leans back, the horse is likely to hollow his back and grind to a halt slowly, whilst raising his head. Another possibility is the horse dives onto his forehand and leans even more heavily into the reins, as shown in Figure 2.

If leaning back is your strategy when there is speed in the equation, do not be surprised if you get run away with, since your attempt to say 'whoa' is actually - by the laws of physics - saying 'go'! It is just as important to be vertically aligned over your horse as it is to stay forward over your skis. In each case, fear can tempt you to do exactly the wrong thing, so that you create a self-fulfilling prophecy. Furthermore, pushing your seat into the horse's back adds adrenalin to the equation, since the horse with his back hollow and his head up reverts to flight mode.

Figure 2

Other ways in which the torso deforms

Another typical error is to push into the stirrups, which will almost always make your seat bones pop up off the saddle and disappear up into your backside. It is important that you keep your feet light in the stirrups to avoid pushing your seat up and back. Next time you ride, try pushing down into your stirrups at halt or in walk. What happens to your seat bones, torso, thighs and lower legs when you do this? Taking time for these little experiments will help you to understand and recognise the consequences of these mistakes.

If you get left behind, or are tempted to lean back, it helps to imagine that you have a vertical plank of wood stuck to the front of your body. As you come forwards into the halt you need to keep your collar bone, sternum, belly button and pubic bone advanced up to the piece of the wood. Ask yourself, which of these four parts of your body comes away from the vertical plank first? If you lean back then perhaps your collar bone and your sternum will come away. If you tip forwards and round your back your belly button and maybe your pubic bone will come away. Can you keep all four points vertically aligned all the way into the halt?

A halt performed well looks as if the horse suddenly decided to halt of his own accord. During the transition the rider remains upright and appears undisturbed by the deceleration. Achieving this takes practice and thoughtful analysis; however, once you start getting it right the horse can rapidly improve the quality of his transitions. Use feedback from the horse as well as feedback from your own body to home in on the question 'What's the difference that makes the difference between good transitions and bad?' Ask someone to video your transitions, and keep noticing!

5 THE TURNING AIDS

Introduction

We often hear the phrase 'inside leg to outside hand' used as a way to help riders create bend, but this attempts to describe a complex feeling that is open to misinterpretation. It is an example of the 'do X' phenomenon, in which the instructor assumes that the student already has A to W functioning well. We need the A, B, C approach to turning.

After seeing thousands of riders competing at the lower levels over the years I (Peter) have come to the conclusion that a large proportion of riders are focused on the horse's nose or his neck when they think about steering. Turning correctly requires a focus on control of the withers and the balance through the horse's shoulders. The rider can then influence the track taken by the front legs, and the proportion of his weight that goes down each of them. Only when you are able to control the shoulders of the horse should you think about bend. Thinking about bend first will make the shoulders much more wobbly and difficult to control.

At the A B C level the turning aids predominantly utilise the outside aids. If you have read my book, Master Dressage or any of the Ride With Your Mind books, you will know that the horse moves away from any given stimulus. If you make a force within your body from the right to the left, then the horse will move to the left. It is with this premise in mind that we now look at turning.

The Turning Aids

To turn a horse there are a number of aids that must be applied. They are listed below:

1. Your outside thigh increases pressure, with your outside lower leg slightly further back. Think of the 'push' starting where the outside of the thigh meets the pelvis, and where the inside of the thigh meets the seat bone.
2. Your outside hand maintains contact and may come closer to the shoulder. Together your outside seat bone, shoulder,

elbow, rein and hand make a wall that the horse cannot bulge through. Think of the horse stepping to the inside with his inside front leg, instead of leading the way with his nose. Your aim is to stop his wither from acting as a hinge, so that he cannot jack-knife like an articulated lorry (or 18 wheeler). Instead he then turns like a bus.

3. You need to make sure that your shoulders stay directly above your hips. It is tempting to turn your shoulders and perhaps also your pelvis to the inside, but experience shows this causes riders to twist and collapse to the inside whilst pulling back with the inside hand. Keep your chin and midline over the mane, being vigilant about any tendency for your torso to deform.

4. Keep your outside aids as a wall whilst you reach into the inside thigh – keep it snug on the saddle as you think of it pointing in the direction you want to go. You may need to advance your inside seat bone, but it needs to stay close to the horse's spine. These ideas help you avoid the contortions that people go through when asked to 'weight the inside seat bone'. When the turn works well you can give your inside hand whilst doing it - no pulling is required.

Photo 8 – Pushing from the outside angle

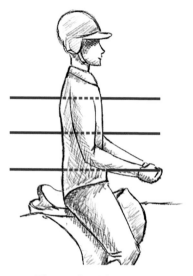

Figure 3 - Skewers

To keep your torso correctly oriented whilst on the circle, imagine that you had 3 skewers going through you, sticking out from both your back and your front. The first skewer passes through you between your shoulder blades, coming out above your sternum. The second goes in through your mid back and out between your sternum and belly button. The third goes into you at the top of your pelvis and comes out between your navel and bikini line.

All three skewers should always be horizontal and parallel. When

Figure 4 - Line Tangent To Circle

you make a turn, keep all of them pointing forwards on a tangent to the circle. This is easier said than done, and riders who are used to twisting to the inside may feel as if they are facing to the outside when they succeed! This piece of imagery is very powerful, and makes clear how you distort your torso when turning. For instance if you twist your shoulders to the inside, the top skewer will point to the inside of the circle. In extreme cases all three skewers point to the inside.

If you rotate your body to the inside as you turn, you are highly likely to also collapse into a C shape, with creases between your ribs and hips on the inside, and the outside of your torso bulging outwards. So imagine your body from the seat bones up as a strong cardboard box with front, back and side panels. As you turn can you keep the panels straight, or do any of the panels deform? For instance, if you collapsed to the right, your right panel would be caved inwards as your left panel bulged outwards.

Figure 5 – Panels of the box

In the six frames in photo 9 you can see the progression from worst to best. Each of the first three frames show a different variation on the theme. Imagine where the skewers would point in each one, and notice how the cardboard box of the rider's torso is deformed. In the final picture you can see that the rider is a good box. All of her skewers lie over the horse's mid-line and would aim along the tangent of her circle.

a. Pelvis sliding left – collapse right   b. Slight collapse left – slide right

c. Sliding left pushing horse   d. Slight lean right but good
   on to its left shoulder

e. Central but right shoulder lower   f. Central axis – thigh leading the way

Photo 9 – Series of frames showing possible errors

Here are some questions you can ask yourself when riding or analysing a video of yourself.

1. Is the front of my body the same length as the back of my body? Have I sucked my stomach in or rounded my back? Is the push forward of my bear down still stronger than my hold on one or both of the reins?
2. Am I focused on steering the horse's nose, or steering his wither?
3. Is my inside hand pulling back as my outside hand goes forward? If so, am I twisting my torso to the inside?
4. Are my skewers, midline, and chin all over the horse's mane and his mid-line?
5. Has the box of my torso deformed into a C shape?
6. Do I have even weight (i.e. 50/50) on each seat bone? If either one lightens, can I keep weight on it by consciously keeping it down and close to the horse's spine?
7. Does my horse speed up or slow down in the turn? If he slows, do I have the brain-space to kick and thrust more (in rising trot, as described in chapter 6)? If he speeds, do I get left behind and pull on the reins? Do I have the courage to keep thrusting and stay 'with' him? You need to be proactive, otherwise you will find yourself tempted to thrust less and/or pull. Keeping the tempo and impulsion the same can significantly lessen any steering aberrations that might otherwise happen.

Typical Problems

My horse falls in

Even though we have said that the outside aids turn the horse, you must always be aware of what the horse is giving you right now. If your horse is already falling in you will need to bring the inside rein a little closer to the shoulder, but do not cross it over the wither. Think of your inside thigh bone like a power hose. Ride rectangles, and aim water through your knee to a distant point that is straight on. Let the aim relax slightly when you want to turn. Then adapt that strategy to the circle.

My horse falls out subtly

Falling out is less well identified by riders, as it often flies under their 'correctness' radar. Many riders who are congratulating themselves on having a correct bend have actually lost control of the horse's front legs, which are falling to the outside of their intended circle. The horse has jack-knifed and used his wither as a hinge.

If this happens, ask yourself "Where am I relative to the horse and where is the horse relative to me?" Typically, when a horse falls out, the rider finds her shoulders to the inside of the horse as her pelvis slides outwards - her skewers and box have gone AWOL! To correct the problem, focus on them, and emphasise the outside aids to bring the horse into alignment. Here are a few consequences of the rider's shoulders being too much to the inside of the horse:

1. The rider may be pulling too much on the inside rein.
2. She may be heavy on the inside seat bone.
3. Her outside seat bone may have lifted up off the saddle and also advanced.
4. As a result, she may have collapsed to the inside and also rotated to the inside.
5. Either leg could feel less secure and effective.

If you have collapsed to the inside you will need to bring your outside shoulder back and down until your 'cardboard box' is not deformed and your skewers remain on the tangent. This correction with your shoulder makes it possible to hold your outside seat bone back and down.

My horse really falls out!

This horse is jack-knifing and quickly running out through his shoulder with his head and neck turned to the inside. There is often an 'Oh no!' moment when the rider realises she will not make the turn and resorts to pulling on the inside rein - which makes the horse jack-knife even more! If you are applying your outside aids to make the horse turn and he is still running out through his shoulder, then you almost certainly have a problem controlling the tempo. If this is the case then improve your turns in walk before you attempt them in trot. Refer to the chapters on the seat (chapter 3) and rising trot mechanism (chapter 6), which will give you more skills to maintain tempo.

My horse pulls on the inside rein and goes straight on.

Horses that do this often have physical issues. Do your best to keep giving away the inside rein and avoid pulling on it as this will put you behind the correct balance point. Instead you must prioritise 'keeping up with' that side of the horse.

Imagine rider and horse as stuffed toys that have lost stuffing in the outside. Most riders are so focused on pulling that they fail to notice the 'emptiness' in the outside of their torso and their horse's ribcage. They have to fill out that side of the horse and themselves and get clarity about the position of their outside seat bone, before they can create a contact on the outside rein and turn effectively.

Sometimes the reason your horse won't turn well is physical and sometimes it is a willful lack of response to your aids. He may also be clueless about what you actually want, especially when your intention and your biomechanics have been in conflict. This is where ground work can really make a difference.

6 RISING TROT MECHANISM

A biomechanically correct rising trot mechanism makes a huge difference to your effectiveness. It enables you to control the horse's tempo, increase impulsion, develop medium/extended paces and steer the horse with greater accuracy.

Some signs that you might need to work on your rising trot are as follows:

1. Your lower leg moves forward and back as you rise. It may go forward as you rise and/or back as you sit.
2. You are unable control the tempo in trot.
3. You feel like the horse throws you out of the saddle.
4. You cannot stop yourself from landing heavily in the saddle.

The Basics of Rising Trot

In rising trot the rider should feel as though she is kneeling up and down with the knee as the centre point of a circle. The pelvis moves along the arc of a circle, defined by the knee as the centre point with the thigh as the radius. Thus the thigh moves like a windscreen wiper on a car. In the photo below we see the rider at the top of the

Photo 10 – Top of the rise

rise.

The next photo shows the same rider at the sit phase of the trot. During the entire time the foot must stay light in the stirrup, with barely any more weight in it during the rise. It is the thigh that levers the rider to the top of the rise and back down again, without her pushing into the stirrup.

Photo 11 – Bottom of the rise

Pushing down into the stirrup will undoubtedly cause the lower leg to move. The stirrup leather is attached to a fixed point and can easily act as a pendulum.

Once your lower leg is too far forwards you will be behind the movement and find it even harder to rise. You will almost certainly land too heavily in the saddle.

Try an experiment next time you ride. Push your weight firmly down into your heels. What happens to your lower leg? What happens to your upper body? What happens to your seat? In a large proportion of cases the rider will see her lower leg swing forward, then her seat will be pushed back in the saddle and her upper body will tip forwards. This would lead to a very unbalanced rising trot.

However, when a skilled rider is at the bottom of the sit her torso will be slightly inclined forwards, even though her heel is still under her hip. This is because her shoulders remain surprisingly still as her pelvis moves forward and back along the arc of the circle. The rider who is upright in the sit is behind the movement; she may well be behind vertical at the top of the rise and she lands too heavily in the sit.

Be careful as you rise to keep the length of your front the same as the length of your back. It is very tempting to lead with your chest and then hollow your back as you rise. This puts your belly button ahead of your pubic bone, so think of your pubic bone leading the way. At first it helps to get the feel of the rising trot mechanism in halt with someone holding your horse. Imagine someone pushing you up with their hand placed on the back of your pelvis and try to lever yourself to the top of the rise using your thighs and core.

The top of the rise will bring your pelvis over the pommel with your body upright and you should be able to balance there without sitting back down. Initially you might find your leg slipping forwards giving you a tendency to fall back into the saddle. Keep thinking of putting weight into your knee, with your foot back and light.

Why rising trot?

In rising trot we are either going from the bottom of the sit to the top of the rise, or vice versa, as the horse makes the jump from one diagonal pair of legs to the other. We are sitting as one diagonal pair of legs is on the ground and at the top of the rise as the other diagonal pair meets the ground. If our rise is too small (only a partial windscreen wiper wipe) the effect could be to reduce the amount of jump that a lazy horse makes. However, if your horse is whizzy and your centre of gravity does not keep up with his, you will become the water-skier to his motorboat.

Rising trot enables us to match the forces acting on our body and to spare our horses from a bouncing rider with a constricting hand. We build valuable skills and our horses build better muscles, carriage and movement - whilst maintaining a good attitude. It also gives us a great tool to control the horse's tempo. By thinking of making a little pause at the bottom of the sit and a little pause at the top of the rise we can cause his feet to stay on the ground for a fraction longer.

You can speed up and slow down the tempo of the trot through controlling the speed with which you go from the bottom of the sit to the top of the rise and vice versa. By using the muscle tone in your thighs you can control how fast the horse moves you. Next time you do rising trot ask yourself whether you or your horse control the speed of your windscreen wiper thighs. Without correct technique you will be at the mercy of whatever speed the horse sets for you. With correct biomechanics you will be able to control the speed of the horse's legs without having to pull on the reins.

7 REIN AIDS

Before we get into any specifics about how to use the reins, we need to warn you against overuse of the hands. Many riders routinely overuse their hands and some use them far too aggressively. Overuse looks like hands that are wiggling, jiggling, or sawing (in constant motion), or like a permanent pull that makes the arm muscles, elbows, wrists or hands 'jump out' to an observer's eye.

Imagine that the reins were suddenly cut, by magic. If the rider would topple backwards she was not in control of her body weight and not matching the forces of the horse's movement. The reins were being used as a counterbalance - not a role we want to inflict on the horse's sensitive mouth or indeed his whole body. But we cannot change this until the rider's body matches the forces so well that she has no need of something to pull against. Only then can she push her hand forward (like the fine example of Charlotte Dujardin).

If, in contrast to the above, you are the kind of rider whose reins are always loopy, try imagining that you have only the reins and bit, with no bridle. Your job is to keep the bit in the corners of the horse's mouth so that it does not fall out and bang against his teeth. That would be by far the more cruel option! Instead you want a steady, consistent contact that is not a pull; both you and the horse can feel the bit in the corners of his mouth.

Very often the rider's hands are controlled by unconscious habit patterns that come into action unbidden. We manipulate the world with our hands, and have a much larger area of the brain dedicated to them than to our core muscles, pelvis, thighs etc. But our hands cannot solve our riding problems. Often they are overused because they are the rider's only tool to 'get the horse on the bit' - especially when she thinks this is primarily about the position of her horse's head.

In the resources section of this book are links to useful videos and articles that talk about 'on the bit', and through these you will see that it is not about getting the horse's head down.

It is not true that one should never use the hands, but they are always used for a specific correction, in a specific moment in time, chosen consciously. After that the hand should go back to still, steady contact, as if the reins were solid rods and the rider could use them to push the horse's head forward.

Next time you ride; check out your hand use. Do you move your hands without you realising? It might even be that if you look down at your hands they became still - so you will only see what they are really doing on a video. Are they level and are your thumbs uppermost? Is one rein longer than the other? Do one or both hands jiggle? Can you choose to use your hands and then go back to a quiet, still contact? Do you ride in 'permanent pull'? What would happen if someone cut the reins? What situations increase the use of your hands?

Pulling Back

In the vast majority of schooling situations we should assiduously avoid pulling backwards on the reins. This means that our body has to be matching the forces of the horse's movement, giving us no need to use the reins as a counter-balance. This is a huge demand, which defines the rider as an athlete and keeps her work ethical.

It is possible to increase the pressure on the reins without pulling backwards. Pulling is analogous to participating in a tug-of-war and of course if one team lets go of the rope the other team would fall backwards! Like rider and horse, the teams are counterbalancing each other, so if the horse were to suddenly release the pressure, the rider's hands would come back even more, giving the horse a further pull in the mouth. If the rider suddenly released the pull, the horse would have to find his own balance without outside 'assistance'.

Passive Resistance as an Increase in Pressure

Imagine once again the two teams holding either end of the rope, but now they have been told that they have to keep the rope taut and maintain a moderately firm tension. They have also been warned that someone will cut the rope in the middle in an unexpected moment. The challenge is now to stay upright and not fall over, even though there is some tension in the rope. This would require a very different attitude to the original tug-of-war!

This is an analogy for a passive resistance. To passive resist, or increase the pressure on the reins, the rider can do the following:

- Press the thumb down more on the top of the rein. (photo)
- Bring the shoulder blades closer together.
- Increase the amount of bear down/forward/out to stabilise the body.
- Bring the elbows more in towards the torso (not backwards)
- Widen the hands a little, whilst bringing the fingernails slightly up.

All of the above strategies have the bonus that if the horse were to yield to the pressure, the rein would become lighter and the rider would stay in place, meaning that no pulling back would happen.

Photo 12 - Thumb on the top of the rein.

The Turning Rein

Turning is another place where riders often pull back, usually on the inside rein. But this should not be used in a backwards action: it should come more to the inside, with the fingernails coming slightly up. The arm will pull rather than passive resist if the fingernails go down and the knuckles point up, and also if the elbow comes back. Again we could ask what would happen if someone were to cut the rein. If your hand would fly backwards then you are certainly pulling back.

Move your hand to the inside, keeping it on the same horizontal plain, and obeying the rules above. You will find that the pressure on the horse's mouth increases a little, but in a controlled way rather than through a backwards pull. The latter would be much more likely to make the horse jack-knife.

Look at the diagram to the left. This shows what happens when your elbow remains in the same place and your forearm/hand moves to the right. You can see that the hand is now further back and thus able to increase pressure on that side of the mouth. As long as you are stabilising your upper arm, shoulder and core, this will be a pressure increase not a pull back.

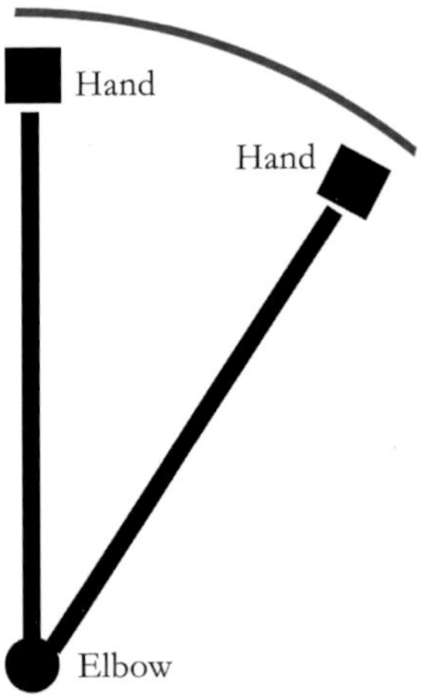

Hand

Hand

Elbow

Figure 6

This is the vital element that separates highly skilled riders from the majority, who, despite their best intentions, would concurrently lean back, hollow or round their back, and/or rotate to the inside as they asked for the turn. These distortions would cause the use of their arm to morph into a pull. The rider has to stack herself up over the horse's long back muscles with tremendous accuracy and stability for an opening rein to work as it should (and to be as easy and effective as most books imply). This element of building skill is an important learning curve for all of us - on one side if not both.

The Indirect Rein

When the horse's shoulder is bulging and falling in or out on a turn, it is also possible to bring the hand and rein closer to the neck to help control this. If the horse were falling out you would bring the outside rein closer in towards the neck, and if he fell in you could bring the inside rein more towards the neck. It is important not to cross the hand over the wither.

The indirect rein is very instinctive and in reality it is a 'sticking plaster correction' that does not really get to the root of the problem. The rein works better when used in conjunction with seat bone, thigh and torso corrections. If the rider does not realise this, she still has a lot to discover about how the rider/horse interaction works!

The bottom line is that as the rider learns how to 'rearrange the stuffing' in her own and the horse's bodies (so that neither of them bulge on one side whilst emptying the other), so she becomes able to counteract the unwanted force that the horse would like to make in one direction. She has to keep her torso really well stacked up over the horse's long back muscle and in her refusal to be distorted she becomes able to take the distortions out of the horse, and to steer him from her body, with virtually no rein.

8 STRETCHING IN WALK

It is extremely important to train your horse to do good stretching in walk, reaching forward and down through his neck. This cannot happen unless he lifts his back and indeed elongates his whole top line - even his hamstring muscles (above his hocks) have to stretch to keep his hind legs reaching under him in each step.

Free walk on a long rein is both a good training tool and proof of the horse's relaxation. It is easy to underestimate the difficulty of this exercise and riders often have the stretch with no activity, or activity without enough stretch. Any tightness in the horse will show up through the lack of one of these elements. There is a reason why it usually has double marks in dressage tests!

When training my horses I (Peter) make stretching in walk a top priority. I start my sessions with this and make a point of riding changes of rein across the diagonal, moving from medium walk to free walk and back again. I focus on smoothly taking up the contact from free walk back to medium walk. This is a proof that my horse follows the contact, neither snatching at it when it is released, nor tensing as I take up the reins.

Tips for training

One basic prerequisite for success is the way your horse walks on from halt. If he raises his head and marches off with his front legs, he takes that first step by lengthening the chain of muscles along his belly and the underside of his neck. He probably does the same in each successive step and when this is an ingrained habit, stretching over his top-line is next to impossible.

In the first step from halt to walk, notice whether your horse begins with a front leg whilst lifting his head, or if he steps firstly with his hind leg, without lifting his head. Work on head lowering in your ground work and make the transition into walk only when his head is down. Pay really close attention to how he takes that first step and notice if pushes his weight down into his chest and the root of his neck as he raises his head. When you can mitigate this and can get him to step from his hind leg with his top line reaching, you will be starting to train the correct habit. Your next task is to transfer this to your ridden work.

Another basic prerequisite for a good free walk on a long rein is the percentage of attention that the horse pays to his rider. When you ride are your horse's ears pricked forwards, or do they mostly point out sideways? This difference determines if his focus of attention is primarily external or internal. A horse that is looking at the scenery and barely paying attention to the rider will usually be too preoccupied to stretch down!

How your horse reacts to the contact is also important for stretching. Aim to ride so that he is always seeking contact and will reach towards it as you allow your hands forward a little. When you ask for stretching in free walk, lighten your seat, putting more weight in your thighs as you slowly allow with the contact. This will encourage stretching over his back. Another tactic is to create a small bend to the inside and then allow the hand forward. As your horse straightens his neck he may also follow the gentle release of contact.

Photo 13 - A photo from a recent clinic shows the rider encouraging stretching by lightening the seat. Here the rider needs to keep the hands more level and a little higher making a straight line down the arm, down the rein and to the bit

Finally, the main skill needed for stretching in walk is ability to influence the horse's back. A rider who can encourage a horse to lift through his back and seek the contact will find stretching easier to train. This skill is also known as getting your horse 'on the bit': but his head and the bit are merely the end points of chains of muscle that involve his whole body.

Due to the negative connotations associated with incorrect bit and rein use, we prefer the term 'the seeking reflexes'. This is because when the horse's whole body is brought into good carriage, he will lift his back seeking contact with the rider's seat and concurrently stretch his neck seeking contact with the bit. He will deepen his breathing, engaging his core and expanding his barrel to seek contact with the rider's thighs.

To go beyond the basics and find out more about how the seeking reflexes work visit **theskilfullrider.com** for some free videos.

9 UPWARD TRANSITIONS

Good upwards transitions are dependent on the movement pattern your horse chooses when asked to go more. Horses who lengthen their underneath and march off with their front legs are using a pattern that will make a hollow transition inevitable.

As with downward transitions, the challenge is to not let your torso be deformed by the forces acting on it. You are now asking your horse to 'change gear' and/or to accelerate. Metaphorically speaking, the rug will go out from under your feet when he accelerates and you need to prevent yourself from either pulling on the reins to save yourself, or toppling back (via the hinge at the waist and/or the hinge at the hip). This would make you incongruent to the horse, since you are saying 'go' and 'whoa' at the same time. Also, the physics of your interaction with him are altered when your centre of gravity falls back. He *cannot fail to* react to that and the contortions could be both physical and emotional.

The answer to staying 'with' him as he accelerates is to bear down/forward/out, which creates a force within your torso that acts from the back to the front. It is important that you keep sitting still and prevent yourself from shoving with your seat, since makes you fall back. Make the transition on an out breath, and deliberately bear down.

Think of this like revving your engine as you build up to the leg aid that asks him to move off. Feel as though you are pushing the back of your body towards the front of your body and the front of your body towards your hands. Then keep that feeling in every subsequent step, so that you are, in effect, hopping along on the space-hopper or hippity-hop. You are then matching the forces of his movement in each step of each gait. It is a huge demand and the secret of really skilled riders.

The horse must also be 'off your leg'. This means that he is ready to respond to a light leg aid and does so as if he were saying 'Yes Ma'm'. If your horse is 'dead to the leg' an upward transition can easily degenerate into kicking and shoving. Good groundwork training is important here and when your horse moves off well from a light whip tap use the same aid when you mount, increasing the intensity of the taps if you need to. Next, use a light leg aid and quickly assess if you need to follow it with whip taps. Your leg aid should be like a light slap that rebounds off the horse's side. Think of your calf and foot like a wooden boot tree inside your boot and move them inwards as one unit (hopefully with no lifted heels or turned out toes), whilst remaining still from the knee up. This too, is easier said than done.

In general it is better for the horse to make a smooth upward transition than a quick one. If you are training your horse to stay in the seeking reflexes, with his back lifted and his neck reaching into the rein, then you should allow him some time to work out how to achieve this in his body. If you were to insist on a quick transition, the horse would choose his most dominant pattern to complete it. At some stage, though, he needs to learn to make prompt transitions whilst staying in good carriage.

Realise that you also need to be aware of the level of energy your horse has in the gait he is currently in. If you wish to go from walk to trot, he needs to be marching along in walk and for this to happen he has to take your leg aids seriously. If you are willing to nag him, you are in effect telling him that your leg aids have no meaning and that there is no consequence for ignoring them. He will never take your leg aids any more seriously than you take them yourself - in fact many riders are barely conscious that they are doing them, yet they somehow expect their horse to consciously obey them. (Is that crazy, or what?)

Canter Transitions

Learning to make a good canter transition can be quite an ordeal for some riders. Many get so desperate that they throw everything they have at the transition, with their whole body getting involved. It is important to think of the transition as a gear change and not as an increase in speed. This means that you want to minimise any acceleration in trot as you prepare for canter.

Canter is not a single aid made in an instant, but a series of aids. Firstly you move from rising to sitting trot, which you need to be able to maintain for a few strides before the strike off. This could already be making a big demand on your skills. Secondly you make a light touch with your inside leg where it normally lies. This is used to prepare the horse and to make sure that he has enough energy. Next you bring your outside leg back, giving a second or two between the inside and outside leg aids. The sequence of legs in canter is outside hind leg, inside hind leg and outside foreleg as a diagonal pair, and finally the inside foreleg. Your outside leg aid is most likely to influence him to canter in that sequence and make the correct strike off. After giving the initial aids it is important that you do not hold your legs against him.

You should also make sure that your outside seat bone is back. Especially if you sometimes get canter strike offs on the wrong lead, think of looking over your outside shoulder so that your skewers (see chapter 5) point out of the circle. Realise that canter is the four-legged equivalent of skipping: in humans one leg is always in front of the other and in horses the inside hind and front legs are always in front of the outside legs. If you do not have the inside of the box of your torso in front of the outside, you are suggesting the opposite pattern and inviting the wrong strike off.

With young and inexperienced horses (as well as struggling riders), it can really help to have a voice command that you have set up on the lunge. If you have become anxious or frantic about the canter transition, start to treat it as an experiment. Your aim is to find out if you can apply the aids for canter and keep everything else still. Can you keep breathing, remain upright, keep your hands pushing forward and only apply the necessary aids? Clear your mind of all else and do not worry about making or not making the transition: focus instead on the challenge of maintaining your alignment and breathing.

Slow the trot if the horse rushes off and ask yourself if you fell back into water-ski position whilst giving the aids. It is important that you do not chase the horse into canter; the challenge is to get the outside hind leg to make the jump underneath him that begins the canter sequence. Sometimes, if the horse is not very responsive to the outside leg, a small tap with the whip as you apply your outside leg will be enough to make the jump happen.

10 PATIENCE & PROGRESS

Are you unconsciously incompetent?

This might sound like a rude question; however all of us are, to some degree, *unconscious of our incompetence*. We are all unaware of habits (which are repeated patterns in the way we fire our neurological 'wiring') that limit our success one way or another. For some people that is an OK state to be in: they are happy with their current level of skill and have no ambition to change. Others have a nagging feeling that they could ride better, but do not want to risk the emotional upset of being pulled apart by a coach.

You may well be one of the many riders who fear the stage beyond being *unconscious of your incompetence*. Here you become *conscious of your incompetence* - you begin to know what your mistakes are and have an inkling (at least) of just how bad they are! This is often a difficult and traumatic time, as we have to completely unpick our once-presumed competence and replace it with new skills and learned responses. Many riders feel really at sea as they move from the old way of performing a skill to the new way.

Once riders have been working on their issues for a while they start becoming *consciously competent*. They have to focus on choosing new patterns over old, but over time they begin to do a relatively good job of holding together their new skill set. This takes commitment and the ability to keep 'hanging in there' and staying focused. You have to be extremely diligent to stop the old habits from creeping back in and it often pays to stop and start again - setting yourself up for success rather than letting your ride degenerate your old ways of doing it wrong. It pays to practice the patterns you most want to ingrain!

Finally, after enough practice, the new skill set becomes the habit that you choose on 'autopilot'. By then you have become *unconsciously competent,* and can perform the new skill without having to think about it. This is how you drive your car - although a lesson with an advanced driving instructor might well render you conscious of your incompetence and put you back into the cycle of learning. In any sphere of expertise, knowing about the four stages can help you get through the cycle without tearing your hair out and giving up on yourself as a bad case!

Retraining.

When faced with retraining a horse - or correcting the flaws that almost inevitably creep in despite our best attempts to train our horses - we have to realise that the way the horse moves is embedded into his very being. His habits determine his current movement patterns and muscle structure. It is primarily his neurological 'wiring' and secondarily his muscle development that support and perpetuate the way he moves.

To get to the root of this, it can feel like you are undoing the very way the horse goes and you may feel like he gets worse initially. For example, consider a horse that is hollow, tight through the back and somewhat high in the head carriage with a shortened neck.

The type of difficulties the rider would experience are: generalised tension, an inconsistent tempo, and sometimes a lack of energy as the horse takes shorter steps with the hind legs. Stretching in free walk on a long rein would be difficult, as would stretching in trot, and over-tracking/tracking up in walk and trot.

This horse needs to be taught to reach over its back, over its neck, and into the rider's hand. His core and his stomach muscles would have to become much more actively engaged - they, and the connective tissue that surrounds them, have been 'locked long' where his back and crest have been 'locked short'. He would need to develop greater freedom through his body and to increase his flexibility. This is little short of retraining the entire way that he moves - and inevitably, we also have to address the 'mind-set' that goes with it!

You as rider are asking him to explore uncharted territory. Perhaps he never realised that there were movement possibilities outside of his familiar restrictions - he arrived on planet earth and trotted off in that way. Or perhaps he has (in effect) been punished in the past for adopting postures that allowed more correct and powerful movement. His rider probably had no intention of doing this, but her riding probably could not 'match' and support the freedom and flexibility inherent in the desired movement pattern. So, metaphorically speaking, she put the lid on it.

Either way, new signals need to be sent from his brain to his muscles, which then need time to adapt to a new movement style.

Eventually he will become 'unconscious of his new competence'; but at the beginning of this process it may be an act of courage for him to step out of his familiar constrictions.

The horse has to firstly consider - and then actively embrace - a letting go of the old way of going. Even with the most skillful rider, this would then be followed by a period of awkwardness and instability as he wavered between the old way and the new way.

This might sound just like the learning cycle for riders and indeed it is. Change can often feel weird, scary and uncomfortable to both people and horses. This effect is amplified when we as riders feel that we are losing gains that we thought we had already made; but this is the price of discovering that something more fundamental was missing. It can take great mental fortitude to step back and leave behind our own artificial deadlines and goals. It is a sign of huge integrity when a rider puts aside her ego and works on herself as a way to work on her horse.

Three Ways You Could Be Preventing Progress

1.   What is, is. Wishing will not make it different. Whatever is currently happening in your training, whatever struggle you are having, you need to apply reason and research to the problem. Regardless of how much we all wish or hope our horses will change, this leads to 'more of the same', to frustration and often to blaming the horse. We need to seek help as we work on our riding and also to investigate the horse's physical issues (including teeth, back, saddle fit etc.). Only then can we learn the skills and knowledge that we need to improve both ourselves and our horse.

2.   You cannot jump from A to Z. Bring your horse on in small increments, challenge him in small amounts. It is very easy to think "Right! That's enough of this baby stuff, let's try shoulder-in". I have seen riders on unbalanced horses hauling them around on 10m circles, or riders attempting lateral work with a horse who is stiff through the back. Others attempt lengthened strides when the horse has no cadence and impulsion in the trot. Move from 20m circles to 15m circles, and make sure a judge would score you at least a 7 before

moving on.

3.   Beware your hubris. Be prepared to unpick your work, go back to basics, learn new skills, change your way of riding and seek help. Read more, and keep a beginner's mind. Never skip the basics. 'Oh I know that already' is a quick way to miss vital information that could hold the key to your problem. Accept and learn more about where you are now. When you become conscious of your incompetence you discover what it is that you do not know and you will uncover the missing pieces that you need to move forward. Good luck!

11 LEARNING RESOURCES

Bonuses

You can now get access to some additional videos and bonuses to go with this book Master Dressage - The Basics.

The bonus page is available at

https://masterdressage.co.uk/the-basics-bonus/

The password needed to access the page is: thebasics5

Blogs

Head on over to http://www.masterdressagelessons.com for lots of free articles and information about Master Dressage.

Visit http://www.mary-wanless.com for access to articles and rider biomechanics information.

Monthly Membership Site

Visit http://www.riderbiomechanics.co.uk/ and get monthly lectures, videos and articles.

Videos

There are lots of free videos on both the Ride With Your Mind and the Master Dressage YouTube channels.

http://www.youtube.com/ridingbiomechanics

https://www.youtube.com/user/MasterDressageNow

The Naked Truth Of Riding DVD Set

These DVDs are unique in their way of combining rider biomechanics and 'reactivity training'. Used together, these paradigms eat into the catch 22 that 'until the horse goes right the rider cannot sit right and until the rider sits right the horse cannot go right.' The results are profound, as illustrated in the changes made by the riders' themselves, and within Heather Blitz's riding and commentary.

DVD 1 is a talk given my Mary Wanless on Language and Learning, explaining why elite riders cannot describe their skill accurately in words and why riders so often get stuck on a plateau. Mary offers suggestions for ways of learning that ensure continual progress.

DVD 2 works in the arena with a group of 4 club level riders. After assessing and realigning the riders and then doing some teaching to confirm those changes, Heather then rides 2 of the horses.

DVD 3 works in the arena with a group of 3 slightly more advanced riders, assessing and realigning them and then doing some teaching before Heather rides 2 of the horses.

DVD 4 works in the arena with 2 more advanced riders and again after realigning and teaching, Heather rides both horses.

The descriptions used by both Mary and Heather, the analysis of the issues presented, and the changes in the horses, present some fascinating new ways of thinking that speak for themselves.

Go to the product tab from www.mary-wanless.com to see more about this groundbreaking DVD set.

On The Bit Lecture Series

Renowned rider biomechanics coach, Mary Wanless BHSI BSc, author of the Ride With Your Mind books and DVDs held a series of Webinars going into detail about getting your horse 'On The Bit' and into the seeking reflexes. All 6 lectures are now recorded and available for viewing.

Lecture 1 On The Bit – The Seeking Reflexes
Lecture 2 On The Bit – 3 Dimensions (i.e. the rider's task in the planes of up/down, back/front, side/side)
Lecture 3 On The Bit – The Mental Problem
Lecture 4 On The Bit – Troubleshooting – common horse problems
Lecture 5 On The Bit – What can prevent it from working?
Lecture 6 On The Bit – Through gaits and transitions

Plus you get supporting videos for each lecture and other goodies along the way. At only £10 per lecture it's way more value than a lesson, plus you get actionable steps to take away from each lecture to try on your horse. Once your payment has been made you will be directed to your membership area where you can watch all 6 webinars and their supporting videos.

For Booking and More Information Go To

https://theskillfulrider.com

Master Dressage – Edition 2

If you liked Master Dressage Edition 1, which held on to the #1 spot on Amazon in its category for over 3 months, you will love Master Dressage Edition 2.

Master Dressage Edition 2, will be in full colour, expanded with additional chapters, more photographs with a great layout and fully edited.

Like my Facebook page www.facebook.com/masterdressage to be kept up to date with the latest news on the release of the book.

Feel free to contact me at support@masterdressage.co.uk

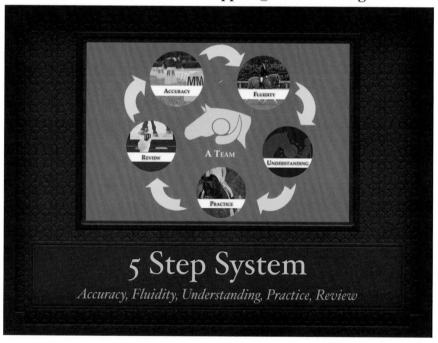

About The Authors

Peter Dove is the #1 Best Selling Author of "Master Dressage - Ride more beautiful tests, get higher marks and have a better relationship with your horse". Check out the 40+ 5 Star Reviews on Amazon for the 1st Edition.

Peter Dove has been riding, teaching and learning dressage for over 25 years. In the 15 years he has been at East Soley EC2000 he has judged and taught combined, some 9000 riders competing at intro to elementary level and beyond. Over the 15 years he has developed systematics ways of explaining how to improve results competing at dressage. www.masterdressage.co.uk

Peter is taught by Mary Wanless BHSI and considers her teachings of rider biomechanics to be one of the main keys to success at all levels of riding and is forever in her debt for all she has taught.

Peter is also a professional computer programmer, photographer and magician. He lives in Chilton Foliat in the UK, married to Emma Dove with two beautiful children Milly and Edward. He is currently studying for his Maths degree with the Open University.

Mary Wanless BHSI BSc is an internationally renowned coach, and is the author of the 'Ride With Your Mind' books, which have been translated into many languages. She has also authored 8 DVDs. She coaches riders at all levels, from relative novices to two of the top twelve US dressage riders, and some of the Canadian eventing squad. She has B.Sc. degrees in both Physics and Applied Sports Coaching, and holds the BHSI certificate.

Her coaching career in the USA began in 1991 with an invitation to speak at the California Dressage Society annual meeting. She has also